Colors

Illustrated by Clare Beaton

World Book

This edition published exclusively in the **My First Books** set by
World Book Publishing, 525 West Monroe Street, 20th Floor, Chicago, Illinois 60661, USA
© 1996 b small publishing

For information on other World Book products, call **1-800-255-1750, ext. 3771.**

green

white

red

black

pink

blue

orange

gray

yellow

brown

purple

A guide to sharing this book with your child

- This book will help your child recognize colors and learn that there are many different colors, each with a different name.

- Talk about the color on each page, and ask your child to find the objects which are that color.

- Point to each word as you read it, and move your finger along as you say it.

- Ask your child what the teddy bear in each picture is doing.

- Ask your child if he can think of anything else that is the same color as the picture?

More things to talk about and do together

- Talk about favorite colors.

- Talk about all the colors around you—in the room, around the house, and outdoors.

- Put together a "color collection" of toys, household items, or pictures from magazines. Introduce just one color at a time.

- Read rhymes and stories that have a color theme, such as *Little Red Riding Hood*.

- As you help your child dress himself, ask him the color of each article of clothing as he puts it on.

- Encourage drawing and painting and talk about the colors your child has used in his pictures.